A river flows with constant force
carving as she meanders
on an ever changing course
gathering verses to replenish
the thirsty souls along her shore.

The River Muse
Journal

The River Muse

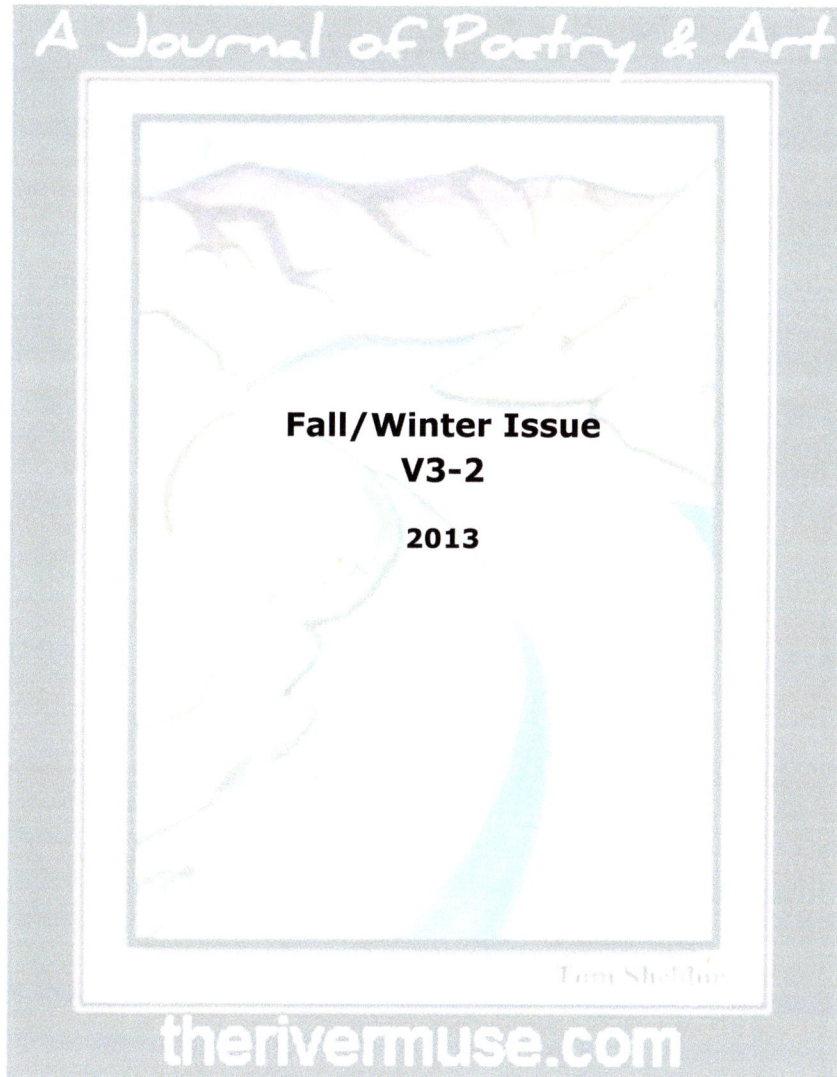

A Journal of Poetry & Art

Fall/Winter Issue
V3-2

2013

therivermuse.com

The River Muse

Journal

Printed in the United States of America

ISBN: 978-0615903774

Twowolvz Press
Stillwater, MN

TWOWOLVZ PRESS

V3-2

Inside this Issue:

Features:

Beverly Bonn Jonnes (poet)

Samantha Fletcher (photographer)

Poetry by:

Terry Wolverton

Russell Buker

Tommy Blackwolf

Marion Friedenthal

Beverly Bonn Jonnes

June Kim

Guy Beining

Jose Varghese

Table of Contents

Introduction

Voices from Around the World

Welcome to the first printed publication of *The River Muse*. A Journal of poetry and art that publishes two seasonal issues a year in print and kindle. *The River Muse* was founded online as *The River* in 2011 by poets and artists. Today, the journal is produced by a creative and talented team from around the world. The journal began as a weekly publication with columns and a handful of followers and quickly grew with material and visitors reaching over 50,000 views. Now, *The River Muse* marks her first print issue of poetry and photography with Volume 3 Issue 2.

The goal of *The River Muse* is to provide the creative through art and poetry for the aesthetic pallets of our readers. The works are from artists and poets locally and all around the globe. In addition, *The River Muse* provides a platform for the emerging and already known poets and artists by showcasing their work in an open and fair publication.   http://therivermuse.com

The River Muse is a *Twowolvz Press* publication.*

* Twowolvz Press is a small press dedicated to encouraging and fostering the imaginations of the youth along with the artistic and literary efforts of artists and writers locally and worldwide through publication, contests, and projects. *Twowolvz Press* publishes poetry chapbooks and *The River Muse*.

Dedicated to Artists and Writers from all Around the World.

-River Urke

Bleak by Samantha Fletcher (cover)

I use photography as a means of showing others how I perceive the world around me; I do not look to recreate scenes exactly how I saw them at the time, instead I am looking to recreate the mood or feeling which I experienced whilst I was there. I also adore nature and being outside, and these are consistent themes in my work. I try to perceive the light, or optimism, in every situation no matter how bleak it might appear; this message is something which I strive for frequently in my photography – a sense of hope in the darkness.

-Samantha Fletcher

Featured Poet

Beverly Bonn Jonnes

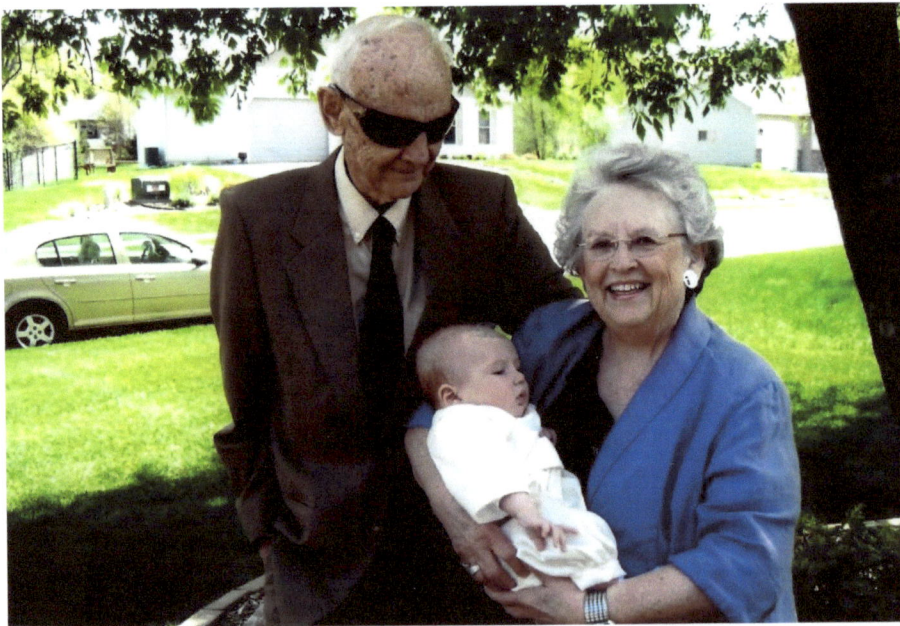

I was born in Montevideo, Minnesota, in 1932 and attended Antioch College in Ohio for two years. I married Nelson Jonnes in 1951. Starting in 1952, we lived and worked in Ethiopia for three years. After our fourth child entered first grade and was, therefore, in school all day, I returned to college and graduated from the University of Wisconsin at River Falls in 1968. For 20 years, I taught fourth through sixth grades in the Stillwater, MN area, where I still live. I was widowed in 2011. I am a grandmother of eleven, great-grandmother of three, happy reader, passionate poet, and friend of lakes / trees / birds / music / and conversation. I started writing poetry after my retirement from teaching and have written every day since. Approximately 80 of my poems have been printed in midwest literary journals and anthologies. Currently, I'm in three local writing groups.

Interview

Recently, I had the pleasure of spending a beautiful Autumn afternoon with the poet Beverly Bonn Jonnes. A woman of exceptional word usage and a sense of humor all would love. We sat eye to eye talking about the world of words and the magic of memories. I asked if Bev could describe poetry in three words.

Beverly: I hope you will allow four words, River, because four words come to mind: discovery, communication, music, exaltation.

Every year, I am more aware of how little I know, but I continue to circle the unknown and try to make sense of it. Reading poetry and writing it sometimes allow me to blow right through the cobwebs in my brain, opening lighted pathways to the possible.

and the possibilities were endless. Bev tells me she has written over 6,000 poems. I ask, When did you begin writing poetry?

Beverly: At the age of ten or eleven, I spent a weekend in a frenzy of writing rhymed poetry. I'd write a poem and then dash into the living room to read it to my parents, who I later discovered were very amused. I remember one line: "I danced with the wind one midnight past." As a sixth grade teacher, I read poetry and taught it, but it wasn't until I retired that I began to write it again. I was watching a television program in which Bill Moyers was interviewing poets, and suddenly I realized that I'd been writing poetry in my head for years. It was an epiphany that sent me to the typewriter, and I have been writing every day since.

Do you have a particular routine or do you write on a whim?

Beverly: I usually write first thing in the morning at the computer in my study. Until recently, I lived in a large house, and my study was on the third floor overlooking the trees and a lake. My friendly crow, Lovely, often stopped by to chat. I prefer computer writing to handwriting because I can more easily keep up with my thoughts and images. However, I don't always have my iPad with me, so I jot down bits and pieces on scraps of paper. I've tried storing a few lines in my head, but I usually forget them before I have a chance to record, proving to me that these words are the opposite of deathless.

Every artist has a muse. A feeling or thing that inspires them to create. What is yours?

Beverly: I spend a lot of time living comfortably in my head, and there are many voices there: friends and relatives living and dead, real and imaginary. Only some of them are human.

Do you have any advice to pass on to a fellow poet?

Beverly: It is surprising to me that some of the would-be poets I've met report not reading much poetry. I would encourage them to immerse themselves in both the classics and the work of modern poets. I would also recommend that they not wait for inspiration to fall on their heads. It amazes me how lines can emerge when I don't have a "good idea" but have bothered to put my hands on the keys.

Interview Conducted by River Urke

Butterflies

Floating at speed of sound, I consider
unexpected butterflies:

thick clouds of small, yellow sulfurs obscuring
our flowered bushes...

the chaos butterfly...

the Siberian crater formed
when a comet exploded, leaving a butterfly of charred
birch trees—fanned-out limbs for wings,
upright trunks for the body.

Thoughtless words, too,
are such butterflies. Thin and short,
they flutter off the tongue to form human craters,
to cause changes in our weather.

Bev at three

The Count

Perhaps
counting is reassuring:

1 - 2 -3, and all is accounted for...
6 for you, 6 for me...
10 little jobs to earn the reward of reading 10 pages...
16 tulip bulbs in a row in the garden.

As I prepare the soil—
    plant,
        tamp,
            water,
                admire—
I realize
I'm counting at random again

as if every movement
is one full step in the deep weaving of here and now,
every tick of time
a blessing.

Lucid As a Dream

Darkest fury and flash do refuse to move on
from Minnesota to Wisconsin, have blown up
and away in a morning storm over the river between.

And all that's left to savor is fresh light,
light that seems to know we're watching as it
thickens, thins, stretches from almost solid to whisper,

appears creamy and then slyly transparent,
smells of fish and spruce before it suddenly has
a brand new scent we can almost catch as it swirls,

almost agree we remember from dreams
recalled as edges falling away. We feel power
of owning some small part of creating a different world

from the one perceived at dawn. We desire
to halt this light, catch it on a finger, lick it off
just once, swallow this seeming source of radiance.

Featured Photographer

Samantha Fletcher

Interview

Samantha Fletcher of Manadh Photography is a self-taught photographer from Sheffield, UK. She has been taking photos for about three years. On January 1, 2011, she started a project 365 (where you take a photo every day for a year), and two and a half years later she is still working on this project, quickly approaching day 1000 of continuous shooting!

"I stay motivated by keeping a sketch book and looking at the work of others; something small in someone else's work might spark off a whole chain of ideas."

Samantha's photography journey is not without its challenges, however.

"I am the model in most of my work (because) it's normally easier to shoot regularly if I'm just using myself. (Plus) weather in the UK can be pretty variable, so it's a lot easier to just nip outside than try to plan things."

"I find shooting without natural light quite tricky, although doing a project 365 forces the need for artificial lighting in the winter months, so I will improve at it the more I practice!"

After completing one full year of daily photographs, Samantha was going to stop. Then her boyfriend bought her a mini studio with some lights as a surprise Christmas present which rekindled her interest.

"I love learning. Even if I take a shot I don't think is great, I can take the experience and learn from it."

 Samantha shoots with a Pentax K30 dSLR and uses an 8mm fisheye, Tamron 1:1 90mm macro, Sigma 30mm 1.4 and Tamron 17-55 2.8 lenses, a tripod and a remote shutter.

"I use photography as a means of showing others how I perceive the world around me; I do not look to recreate scenes exactly how I saw them at the time. Instead, I am looking to recreate the mood or feeling which I experienced whilst I was there.

I also adore nature and being outside, and these are consistent themes in my work. I try to perceive the light, or optimism, in every situation no matter how bleak it might appear; this message is something I strive for frequently in my photography – a sense of hope in the darkness."

When not taking photos, Samantha teaches Computer Science and Psychology at a secondary school. She also enjoys knitting, reading books, and being outside exploring new places.

Find more of Samantha's work on Facebook (/manadhphotography) and on her blog (www.manadh-photography.com)

Interview Conducted by Sheila Moore

Bakewell in Mist by Samantha Fletcher

Poetry

I consider myself a poet first and a musician second.

I live like a poet and I will die like a poet.

--Bob Dylan

Terry Wolverton

Tinnitus Lullaby

Is the night swollen with birdsong
or are my cochleae singing
to me again, phantom echo
of sounds I once heard in pre-dawn
India, when trees came alive?

I called you across continents
so you too could hear the music
of birds awakening beside
the temple that glowed like a lantern,
while sacred chants poured from windows,
rippling across dark water.

I've always been lonely. The world
leaves its fingerprints on me,
but all I touch dissolves to smoke,
and I'm left listening only
to the music inside my head.

Approaching Storm by Samantha Fletcher

Russell Buker

Still have

difficulty coaxing the
inert
sense of my November
self

makes me wonder
why

I had stopped in
the first place
to watch you walk
away

in my favorite floral
dress

wait, wait I wanted
to shout
till you turned , came
back

to my, our, agony. I
felt an imaginary cheek
tear

while I stood a static,
indulgent heart simply
pumping waking me
systemically

and still I waited, waited
knowing you're eight hundred
miles and unable to walk the
hand
in hand out in our imaginary
sea

Post ignition

Only with a rude
laugh,
cosmic comic, is it
possible
to regulate oneself
as
mere pollution, light
pollution,
the way undistinguished
pain
works its way into a light
in
ones brain-flashing wince

would that I stopped
evolving
except in crystal. How
simple
life is without any light
playing
off the planes of shear
successive
fractures, crypts, where we
assume
an understanding how much
heat
and cooling out it was that

made us in the first: facets
of
reflecting snow beguiled
with
an unfathomable sense of
what
lies below in the compact
darkness
and what began as a laugh
turns
vague, then pixels to
apprehensive,
solstice to solstice

Tommy Blackwolf

Sands of Time

the wind blows golden pellets of heat carving out a figure
spotted guardians pace as the sculpted body transforms
once dry granules of earth morphed into soft mirages of beauty
a trick perhaps to the untrained eye look deeper still ..magic

she stretches her golden liquid body across the dune
testing the boundaries of this new found transformation
an uncontrollable desire to reach across the plains
to touch all that can be seen to be touched by all that see's

a keeper of the sands of time now wanting to be kept
the silhouette of a child stealing a glance, deciphering reality
feeling the warmth of the desert wondering what tricks it plays
the dunes holding her beautiful form as the cheetahs pant

even the meerkat struggles with this vision
this goddess of sand and time naked before them
the steely wisdom of the great cats glance confirms
the open mind transcends, opening a new chapter

to believe what is seen to see what is believed
reaching out to feel what is or is not there
the child races to her side wanting to be held
looking down his hands fill with the sands of time

T.A.L

Marion Friedenthal

Forlorn

Gelid
extremities,
consumed by illusion
of warmth, swipe at snot-encrusted
noses.
Listless
emaciated remnants of
childhood huddle around
otiose flames.
Street kids.

Cabalistic

Carve
A sign
Before we
All leave this place
Lest we be forgot
In the time still to come.
Secrete our rituals in rock
That all may know we once were here.
Invincible warlocks, hear me now -
Carve a sign before we all leave this place.

V3 - 2

Of a captivating summers day by Samantha Fletcher

June Kim

Koi No Yokan

the knowledge that you will fall into love, not love at first sight but knowing that a
future love is inevitable

At cliffside
river is watching

Snapping photos
as tiny dancers mirror landscapes
out to meet you

Moon and Sun bathe
while knowledge offers me a drink

I see you in the distance of a cloud
as you wash over me

Lullabye

Suckling on the dreams of mothers
in the lineage of their milk

Descended now unto you
the openness of mouth

Rounding corners
exposed flesh
pulling tugging best expressed

Sweetness devours
dripping success

Lay hour head
gently rest

Full moon bellies
seize the day

Milk fed dreams
washed away

Liken to lickin'
surfaces exposed

in order to know self
never to outgrow

Pull, nudge and tug
against a dry expanse
into the lie of day

This desert has left you
high and dry
never did you bother to flower.

The Great American Game, Innocysim

I toured your duty for the Hallmark Cup of Fame
The destiny of the cup was in the leaf,
a charred bitter taste that left you
out in the field
pitching strikes to no man's land
Up-keeping greens on diamond parks
alongside the minefields of second base
We were born to raise our cups to shield the stains
with popcorn peanuts and…
I don't care if I ever come home!

I can no longer capture summer on a tip of a spoon
inside the mind of my ink pen
Nor can I pronounce the ineffable longing
creating pastime to pastime to past time
I begin to lose the sense of where I am
wrapped in a loop of heaping mounds of relish,
inside one nation under god

Another pastime stuck on replay
is on display in the white room next door
They are tucked and lined up ready for action
like figures in a playroom, handle with care.
There are thousands, millions and eons of cups that were taken from
me

I prefer the cup of innocence, with the clip and the piston ready to go
at a moment's sip.

Beverly Bonn Jonnes

Slumber-Party Women

We slumber-party women
talked all night about making changes
in our lives... and now, right now
with the Venetian blinds offering us
a sunrise of watermelon in thick slices,
we've decided today's the day.
Yes, today. Today
          we can do it.

We've recalled how easily the child
slides from tears to wide smiles
at the sight of ice cream or less.
And someone recited the hopeful story
of a woman who heard melodies
in her head, decided to become...
became at last
          a songwriter at 75.

We've decided to elbow the breeze,
deflect it in preferred directions...
to yank out handfuls
and throw them over our shoulders...
to blow that breeze new kisses.
Yes, yes, we can make a change today.
Today's the day.

        We can do it.

Misty morning at Ladybower reservoir by Samantha Fletcher

Guy Beining

felt tongue 176

it is a picture
of no means.
we can't penetrate
the window.
the shine is gone
it is as dark as
what it hides.
there is a brow
in one pane,
3rd from the top.
all those divisions
(12) divide nothing.
someone once grabbed
a slab of darkness
& pinned it
to a wall.
it smelt of guilt
but told us nothing.

felt tongue 178

each corner was
dirtier then the
last one...the
ragman, an oily
figure, deep in fumes
was tricked into one.
lights flickered along
a spaded path which
he had covered up,
leaving the scent
of a century. one
soft scull was left
it had survived
all the bright funerals,
all the sad notes,
having pushed against the
sound of rock onto rock.

V3-2

Jose Varghese

The Dancer And The Dance

From a longing
wordless to the core
you breathe in those colors
that your costume exudes.
Your torso is fluid,
and legs move like reeds
in a river flowing soft.
You slice air to delicious
pieces of dessert
and serve it on ornate china
before my eyes.
I receive solid images
one by one.
A peacock preening its feathers,
just in deep thought
before that
wondrous spread of colors.
A bear letting itself lost
joyfully to wild moves.
A dragon discovering angst
in unbridled display
of lost terrains.
A god whose eyes
are fixed on eternity.
A demon whose limbs
go awry in wild abandon.
A man who sweat inside
many-layered forms.
A sigh that escapes through
your mask, as you struggle to
stay on your feet and make me
believe in the dance.

Biographies
of poets

Terry Wolverton is the author of ten books of fiction, poetry and creative nonfiction. She has also edited 14 literary compilations. Terry is currently collaborating with jazz composer David Ornette Cherry to adapt her novel in poems, Embers, as a jazz opera. She is Affiliated Faculty in the MFA Writing Program at Antioch University Los Angles, and the founder of the Los Angeles based writing center, Writers At Work. www.terrywolverton.com.

Russell Buker recently retired from Shead High School where he taught English and Creative Writing. He has also coached for many years: football, baseball, basketball and tennis Russell has had numerous poems accepted in many publications in the U.S. and in Canada. Also, he has served on the board of editors and written book reviews for Off the Coast Review.

Tommy Blackwolf is a poet, song writer, and musician living in Stillwater, Minnesota. His writings reflect what his eyes have seen and his heart has felt from his home on the streets as a runaway to the arms of his Angel in midlife. Tommy's poetry http://twowolvz.wordpress.com/
Tommy's music http://www.reverbnation.com/tommyblackwolf.

Marion Friedenthal is a poet, writer, and upcoming grandmother living in Johannesburg, Gauteng with her husband.
You can find Marion's work at Bleeding Moon Poetry. ~
http://bleedingmoonpoetry.blogspot.com/

June Kim worked in the Entertainment Industry as a Film Accountant for 25 years. Currently working as Budget Manager for the School of Film & Television at Loyola Marymount University. Rekindling her poetic voice at Loyola with workshops led by Brendan Constantine she was inspired to never stop writing. Currently residing in Los Angeles writing poetry and practicing energy medicine.

Beverly Bonn Jonnes is this issues featured poet. Beverly guesses she has written over 6,000 poems over the last fifteen years. Check out her interview in the beginning of the journal.

Guy Beining There was no biography with the submitted poetry.

Jose Varghese was the winner of last spring's poetry contest. Check out his interview on *The River Muse*.

The River Muse
Journal

V3 ~ 2